Drew Brees

By Adam Boehler and Sabrina Crewe

Crabtree Publishing Company

www.crabtreebooks.com

Crabtree Publishing Company

www.crabtreebooks.com

Author: Adam Boehler and Sabrina Crewe
Publishing plan research and development:
Sean Charlebois, Reagan Miller
Crabtree Publishing Company
Coordinating editor: Paul Humphrey
Editors: Geoff Barker, Kathy Middleton
Photo researcher: Geoff Barker
Proofreader: Wendy Scavuzzo
Designer: Ian Winton
Series design: Ken Wright
**Production coordinator and
prepress technician:** Michael Golka
Print coordinator: Katherine Berti

Produced for the Crabtree Publishing Company
by Discovery Books

Photographs:
Alamy Ltd: Ninette Maumus: p.21
Corbis: Jeff Haynes/Reuters/Corbis: p. 4 (top);
Walik Goshorn/Retna Ltd./Corbis: p. 9; David
Bergman/Corbis: p. 16; Derick Hingle/Icon SMI/
Corbis: p. 17; John G. Mabanglo/epa/Corbis:
p. 18; Tony Medina/Icon SMI/Corbis: p. 22 (top)
Dreamstime/Todd Taulman: cover
Getty Images: Jim McIsaac: p. 6; Harry How: p. 12;
Peter Brouillet/NFLPhotoLibrary: p. 14; Donald
Miralle: p. 15; Kris Connor: p. 26; Sports
Illustrated: p.27 (top)
Photoshot: Joe Rimkus Jr: p.19; Al Diaz/Miami
Herald/MCT: p. 28
Seth Poppel: Seth Poppel/Yearbook Library: p. 10
Shutterstock: Caitlin Mirra: p. 4 (bottom); Debby
Wong: p. 13; Action Sports Photography: p. 22
(bottom); Allen Berezovsky: p. 23; Marc Pagani
Photography: p. 24
Wikimedia Commons: US Navy: p. 1; Tulane
Public Relations: p. 5; Sgt. Michael Baltz: p. 7;
Ian Ransley: p. 8; Michael A. Lantron: p.11;
Derek Bridges: p. 20; Marty Bahamonde:
p. 25; Keith Hinkle: p. 27 (bottom)

Library and Archives Canada Cataloguing in Publication

Boehler, Adam
Drew Brees / Adam Boehler and Sabrina Crewe.

(Superstars!)
Includes index.
Issued also in electronic format.
ISBN 978-0-7787-7616-1 (bound).--ISBN 978-0-7787-7629-1 (pbk.)

1. Brees, Drew, 1979- --Juvenile literature. 2. Quarterbacks
(Football)--United States--Biography--Juvenile literature. 3. New
Orleans Saints (Football team)--Juvenile literature. I. Crewe,
Sabrina II. Title. III. Series: Superstars! (St. Catharines, Ont.)

GV939.B695B64 2012   j796.332092   C2012-906752-0

Library of Congress Cataloging-in-Publication Data

CIP available at Library of Congress

Crabtree Publishing Company

www.crabtreebooks.com   1-800-387-7650

Printed in the U.S.A./112012/FA20121012

Published in Canada
Crabtree Publishing
616 Welland Ave.
St. Catharines, ON
L2M 5V6

Published in the United States
Crabtree Publishing
PMB 59051
350 Fifth Avenue, 59th Floor
New York, New York 10118

Published in the United Kingdom
Crabtree Publishing
Maritime House
Basin Road North, Hove
BN41 1WR

Published in Australia
Crabtree Publishing
386 Mt. Alexander Rd.
Ascot Vale (Melbourne)
VIC 3032

JB Bre

CONTENTS

Words that are defined in the glossary are in
bold type the first time they appear in the text.

Hopes and Dreams

The Super Bowl is one of the biggest sports events of the year in the United States. It is the championship game of the National Football League (NFL). Winning the Super Bowl is the dream of every professional football player.

Meet Drew

Drew Brees is a **quarterback** for the NFL team the New Orleans Saints. In 2010, he led the Saints to victory in the Super Bowl. Behind that victory, there are several stories. One is the story of a team that found hope and leadership. Another is the story of a city that was destroyed and rebuilt.

Drew Brees holds up the Super Bowl trophy after his team's victory in 2010.

In 2005, Hurricane Katrina **devastated** whole neighborhoods of New Orleans.

DRUG FREE ZONE

4

Coming Back Stronger

Yet another story is that of a great sportsman who overcame defeat and injury. All these stories are part of Drew's story.

He Said It

He deserves everything that he has, what he has earned, and what he has coming to him. Everyone knows he's a great football player, but he's also a great guy—fun to be around, very down to earth, and doesn't think he's better than anyone else. . . . He treats everybody the same way.
—New Orleans **running back** Mark Ingram, *Sporting News*, August 2012

Drew Brees gets ready for a new season with the New Orleans Saints.

Role Model

Drew Brees is a hero to his fans and a role model for fellow athletes. He is famous for the good work he does for others. Drew has fought against bullying in schools. He raises money for cancer victims and families in need. Above all, Drew helped rebuild communities after Hurricane Katrina hit New Orleans in 2005.

Drew is also known as a family man, dedicated to his wife and three small children. He has a reputation for having a strong moral character in both his personal life as well as in sports.

Drew poses with wife Brittany and his eldest son, Baylen.

Never Give Up

Drew gives the credit for his success to his religious faith and "never give up" attitude. In 2010, he wrote a book with the title *Coming Back Stronger*. The book is about his life and achievements, but it's also about the challenges he faced along the way.

The second part of the book's title is *Unleashing the hidden power of **adversity***. By adversity, Drew means the hard times and events in life that work against you. He believes you can use those things to improve yourself and make your life better.

Drew is happy to sign autographs for fans. Here he signs a team flag for a Saints fan.

He Said It

See adversity as an opportunity. Remember, experience is what you get when you don't get what you want. . . Seize that adversity and let it make you stronger. Welcome it, and unleash its power.
—Coming Back Stronger: Unleashing the hidden power of adversity, 2010

Rising to the Challenge

Andrew Christopher Brees was born January 15, 1979, in Dallas, Texas. Right from the beginning, everyone called him Drew. And right from the beginning, football was in his blood.

Football in the Family

Drew says he grew up in a very sports-minded family. Both Drew's parents, Mina and Chip, were lawyers, but football ran in the family.

Drew's grandfather, Ray Akins, was a football coach. His uncle, Marty Akins, was an All-American starting quarterback for the Texas Longhorns college football team from 1975 to 1977.

As a child, Drew was teased by other kids about the birthmark on his right cheek. Now fans stick fake birthmarks on their own faces as a tribute to their hero.

He Said It

If you look at pictures of me as a child, you'll see the birthmark, but you'll also almost always see me holding a football or a baseball. As far back as I can remember, football has been a part of my life.
—*Coming Back Stronger: Unleashing the hidden power of adversity,* 2010

Brotherly Bond

Drew and his younger brother Reid followed in the family footsteps. They grew up in Austin, Texas, playing baseball all the time. They dreamed of becoming baseball champions. Reid went on to play baseball in college, but Drew turned to football.

When Drew was seven, his parents divorced. This experience brought him and his brother even closer together. They have always been proud of each other's success.

He Said It

Watching my brother play in Omaha [in the College World Series] in 2005 ranks up there as one of the proudest moments in my life. My brother was living out a childhood dream for both of us.
—Coming Back Stronger: Unleashing the hidden power of adversity, 2010

Drew has encouraged a love of baseball in his sons from an early age.

Capture the Flag

Drew attended St. Andrew's Episcopal, a private school in Austin. The kids there played flag football. Players have to capture a flag, which is a colored strip of cloth, from the player carrying the ball. Flag football, says Drew, develops your skills.

The Chaps

In 1993, Drew went to Westlake High School. He was still playing basketball and baseball, but Drew's football career was about to begin.

TOPS IN TENNIS

At the age of 12, Drew was the number one tennis player in Texas in his age group.

At Westlake High, Drew was an all-round athlete.

Johnny Rogers was the starting quarterback for the Chaps football team at Westlake High. A quarterback has to be smart, quick, and able to throw the ball. When Drew joined the team as a **second-string** quarterback in 1994, Johnny said to himself, "I'm in trouble—I might lose my job."

Quarterbacks are always at risk of injury on the field.

Two Injuries

In 1995, just before the season started, Johnny injured his knee. Drew became the starting quarterback for his team. He led his team through a successful season. Late in the season, however, there was another injury, but this time it was Drew who got hurt. He tore a **ligament** in his knee and had to have surgery. It took a long time to heal. For Drew, it was a turning point. He was determined to come back stronger.

The Next Step

Drew Brees did come back stronger. The Chaps did not lose a single game in 1996. Led by Drew, they went on to win their first state championship. Drew graduated from Westlake High in 1997. He was ready to move on up.

He Said It

The […] injury was a defining moment in my life. I made a decision not to let something negative control my emotions.
—Coming Back Stronger: Unleashing the hidden power of adversity, 2010

Into the Big Ten

Most colleges thought Drew wasn't tall enough to be a big-time college quarterback. But Purdue University in Indiana offered Drew a scholarship. Purdue is in a major **football conference** called the Big Ten. Drew knew it was his best opportunity. In 1997, he set off for Indiana.

Brees the Boilermaker

Drew had to work hard in the classroom, where he studied industrial management. He also worked hard on the football field.

Fans mob Drew Brees in 1999 after the Boilermakers beat Notre Dame's Fighting Irish.

Purdue's team is called the Boilermakers, and Drew wanted to be the starting quarterback. Eventually Drew's hard work paid off. He played in seven games in his freshman year.

A Year to Remember

The following year, Drew became a star. He set single-season records in 1999 in the Big Ten conference in **passing yards** and **touchdowns**. The Boilermakers finished with a record of 9 wins and 4 losses that season and went on to beat Kansas State at the Alamo Bowl. Drew was named MVP (Most Valuable Player) of the game.

1999 was also the year that Drew Brees met Brittany Dudchenko. Brittany was a fellow student at Purdue. The couple met on Drew's 20th birthday.

To the Rose Bowl

In his senior year, Drew led the Boilermakers to the 2001 Rose Bowl. Although the Boilermakers lost to the Washington State Huskies 34–24, the game was a highlight of Drew's college career. By the time he graduated in 2001, Drew had set Big Ten records in passing yards, touchdown passes, total offensive yards, completions, and attempts.

Drew met Brittany in 1999. She was at his side when he received Sportsman of the Year Award in 2010.

She Said It

Who is this young idiot football player who's so full of himself?
—Brittany Brees, when she first met Drew in 1999

Charging Forward

After college, the next step for a successful football player is to be **drafted** into the NFL. In spite of Drew's college successes, NFL teams doubted that Drew could play at their level.

Drew was used to the doubts. He had overcome them in high school and again in college. He was determined to do so again. Sure enough, in 2001, the San Diego Chargers drafted Drew into the NFL.

Drew spent much of his first two seasons on the bench as a backup. He played more in 2003, but the Chargers finished with a 4 wins/12 losses record. In the 2004 draft, the Chargers picked a talented young quarterback named Philip Rivers. Drew knew his job might be on the line. He would have to focus harder than ever to keep it.

Philip Rivers filled Drew's spot as quarterback for the San Diego Chargers in 2005.

Career High

The 2004 season was Drew's best yet in the NFL. He led the Chargers to first place in their division and into the **playoffs**. They lost to the New York Jets in overtime, but Drew was selected to play in the Pro-Bowl, the NFL's all-star game, with the rest of the NFL's best players.

The following season, Drew's personal success continued. He threw for a career-high 3,576 yards. But his team failed to make the playoffs.

HAPPY DAYS

Drew and Brittany traveled to Europe. At a restaurant in Paris, France, Drew proposed to Brittany. They married in 2003.

John Lynch of the Denver Broncos (left) tackles Drew Brees in 2005. Drew's shoulder was injured in the play.

Life Changer

In the last game of the 2005 season, against the Denver Broncos, Drew's career changed quickly. During a tackle, Drew's shoulder on his throwing arm was torn out of its socket. His career with the Chargers was over.

Super Bowl and Beyond

After his injury, Drew Brees had surgery on his shoulder. Four months later, he was throwing again. Drew was no longer in San Diego, however.

To New Orleans

In 2006, Drew signed a six-year contract worth $60 million with a different team. He was now quarterback for the New Orleans Saints. The Saints believed Drew's arm would heal and that he would lead them into the playoffs.

Drew led the Saints to a 10–6 record that year. They won their division and made the playoffs. It was the best season in the team's history. But they fell one game short of the Super Bowl. Drew had turned the team around, but he had not achieved his ultimate goal.

Head coach Sean Payton asked Drew Brees to join the New Orleans Saints.

She Said It

Drew had to get injured for us to leave San Diego and for us to be here. It's one of the greatest things that ever happened to us.
—Brittany Brees, in *USA Today*, July 2007

16

Try and Try Again

In 2007 and 2008, the Saints failed to make the playoffs. Drew knew the most important thing was to improve in 2009. So he focused his strengths. When the season started, Drew and the Saints were ready to win. And win they did.

Drew and the Saints won 13 straight games to start the season. Then the Dallas Cowboys beat them, ending their undefeated streak. But the Saints were the best team in their conference. In the playoffs, they beat the Arizona Cardinals 45–14. They edged out the Minnesota Vikings in overtime, 31–28. The Saints were on their way to the Super Bowl.

SPECIAL YEAR

2009 was a special year for Drew from start to finish. Drew and Brittany's first child, Baylen, was born on Drew's birthday, January 15.

In January 2010, the Saints beat the Arizona Cardinals in the playoffs on their home turf—the Superdome in New Orleans.

Super Bowl XLIV

On his way to the Super Bowl, Drew was **dominant** on the field. He set a new NFL record by completing seven of every ten passes he threw (70.6 percent!), and he was selected for his fourth Pro-Bowl game. But his biggest achievement on the field was yet to come.

Drew directs the play during Superbowl XLIV.

LETTERS FOR NUMBERS

Super Bowl numbers are written in **Roman numerals**. The game in 2010 was the 44th Super Bowl. So it is written as Super Bowl XLIV.

The Super Bowl is the most watched sports event in the United States. On February 7, 2010, more than 106 million people were watching the Super Bowl on television. The Saints met the Indianapolis Colts at the Sun Life Stadium in Miami Gardens, Florida. Peyton Manning, another star quarterback, led the Colts.

Victory

There was much excitement and entertainment on the field. It was very distracting for both teams. At half time, the Colts were ahead. But through it all, Drew and the Saints stayed focused. The Saints kept scoring points and turned the game around to beat the Colts 31–17. It was the first time the Saints had ever won the Super Bowl. Drew was named Super Bowl XLIV Most Valuable Player.

He Said It

When I held up my son, Baylen, after the fourth quarter of Super Bowl XLIV, with confetti streaming down all around us, it was the fulfillment of a dream. But what I've discovered along the way is that the road to success is usually a pretty bumpy one. And there are no shortcuts.
—*Coming Back Stronger: Unleashing the hidden power of adversity*, 2010

Celebration in the City

For the first time ever, the Saints had won the Super Bowl. It was a victory that the people of New Orleans badly needed. Beaten and battered by Hurricane Katrina in 2005, the city at last had something to celebrate.

Drew celebrates with his team and fans during the Super Bowl Victory Parade in New Orleans.

Saints fans and everyone else poured into the streets. The city was alive with music and dancing. Strangers hugged each other, crowds chanted, and brass bands played. If Drew Brees was not already a hero in New Orleans before the Super Bowl, he had certainly become one after.

Saints Fever

In New Orleans, fans continue to take great pride in the Saints. The city's adoration of its football team is sometimes called "Saints fever." Much of the fever is focused on Drew Brees. Some people say, "What would Jesus do?" when they are trying to decide the right thing to do in a situation. Drew's fans replaced Jesus with Breesus. "What Would Breesus Do?" T-shirts appeared all over the city and on the Internet. Brees understood that the phrase shocked some people, but he saw it as a sign of affection from happy New Orleans fans.

Who Dat?

The community of Saints fans calls itself the Who Dat Nation. As the 2010 celebrations continued, the familiar chant was everywhere. The Saints fans and spectators chant, "Who dat? Who dat? Who dat say dey gonna beat dem Saints?"

WHO DAT? NATION

The Saints' Super Bowl victory brought new hope to New Orleans.

NO DOUBT WHO DAT

Many fans and teams have claimed the Who Dat cheer started with them, but there is no doubt that it now belongs to the New Orleans Saints. The team officially adopted the cheer in 1983.

Scandal in the Saints

Drew Brees performed well in 2010 and 2011. He even set new records, but the Saints didn't make it back to the Super Bowl. In 2012, he faced the new season without his **mentor**, head coach Sean Payton. The NFL **suspended** the coach for one year after **scandal** hit the Saints. Four players were also suspended. The team's staff was accused of paying its players **bonuses** to injure opponents on the field.

Drew denied that he had been part of the scandal. At the same time, he wanted to defend his teammates. In a letter to his fans on his website, he said "We owe it to [the young people] to provide the best example of how to behave as professionals."

Sean Payton (right) on the field with Drew in 2012, just weeks before he was suspended.

NFL RECORD

In 2012, Drew broke the NFL record for the highest number of consecutive games (48) in which a player threw touchdown passes. He beat a record set more than 50 years ago by Johnny Unitas.

$100 Million Man

In July 2012, Drew Brees set a record of a different kind. He signed a five-year, $100 million contract with the New Orleans Saints. After receiving $40 million in 2012, Drew is guaranteed another $60 million over the life of the contract. That sum is the largest ever guaranteed to a player in the history of the NFL.

As champions, Drew and the other Saints earn millions of dollars a year.

Growing Family

Life on the home front was busy, too. Since the day that Baylen was held high by his dad at the Super Bowl, Drew and Brittany have had two more children. Bowen was born in October 2010, and Callen was born in August 2012.

As always, a big part of Drew's life continued to take place off the field. His generosity and commitment to helping others is what makes him a true hero.

After the Hurricane

In 2003—years before the Super Bowl win—Drew founded a charity called the Brees Dream **Foundation**. Drew, Brittany, and the foundation have since donated more than $11 million to people and communities in need.

City in Ruins

In August 2005, Hurricane Katrina hit the Gulf Coast of the United States. Winds and floods battered the city of New Orleans. The poorest communities in the city were hit the hardest. Whole neighborhoods were destroyed.

When Drew arrived in New Orleans after the floods, he quickly found ways to help. Soon, the Brees Dream Foundation was helping rebuild those neighborhoods. One Brees Dream project is called Rebuilding Through Brotherhood. The foundation brings college students to New Orleans to build houses with a project named Habitat for **Humanity**.

He Said It

When I visited New Orleans. . . the city was devastated. . . But I just thought, this is a chance to be part of something incredible—the rebuilding of an American city. I felt like it was a calling. Like I was destined to be here.
—*Sports Illustrated*, January 2010

Building the Future

Much of the money Drew raised and donated went into rebuilding schools, parks, playgrounds, and sports fields. It also goes into programs to help kids toward a more hopeful future. A typical project, and one of Drew's favorites, was the Lusher Charter School. The school had been damaged in the hurricane. The foundation gave $750,000 to build a sports field and other facilities. "A lot of times, these kids just need someone to believe in them," said Drew, talking about the kids at Lusher School.

The Superdome, home of the Saints, became a shelter for the homeless when Hurricane Katrina struck New Orleans.

25

Getting Fit, Staying Healthy

Drew helps people get healthy in several ways. In 2010, President Barack Obama appointed Drew to be co-chair of the President's Council on Fitness, Sports & Nutrition. Together with former champion gymnast Dominique Dawes, Drew leads a mission to help Americans get healthy through exercise and good diet.

Dominique Dawes (center) works with Drew to encourage kids to get healthy.

RICE BOWL

For the Rice Bowl Challenge, Drew worked with the United Nations' website FreeRice.com to raise money to feed the hungry. Winners of the online word game received footballs signed by Drew.

Helping Sick Kids

From the start, the Brees Dream Foundation supported the fight against cancer. In addition to all their work in New Orleans after Hurricane Katrina, Drew and Brittany continue to help hospitals and give support to programs for sick kids and for families living with cancer.

Amazing Race

The Brees Dream Foundation hosts an annual "Amazing Race" event in New Orleans. All money from the event benefits children and families in Louisiana and the Gulf Coast. In 2012, the foundation joined forces with another organization. Just Keep Livin was started by actor Matthew McConaughey and his wife Camila Alves to help teenagers stay healthy.

Drew sets an example by working out to stay fit and strong.

He Said It

Drew and Brittany have done such an amazing job supporting youth in the community and Camila and I are excited to participate in the Amazing Race this year. We are all here for one reason and that is the kids.
—Movie actor Matthew McConaughey, 2012

Camila Alves and Matthew McConaughey joined Drew and Brittany to help young people in the Amazing Race.

27

It Gets Better

In 2010, the media were full of reports about teenagers taking their own lives after being bullied in school. Drew spoke up, supporting the anti-bullying campaign "It Gets Better." In a video, Drew told kids "if you're making fun of someone because they're different, then you are no friend of mine."

TRUST YOUR CRAZY IDEAS

The Brees Dream Foundation funds an after-school program called Trust Your Crazy Ideas. It challenges kids to put ideas into action and donates the money to develop projects.

Drew Brees is a true fighter. His determination has kept him at the top of his sport.

Finish Strong

Whatever the future holds for Drew in his football career, he will continue to do what he can to help young people. Drew has overcome difficulties in his own life and ended up stronger. He believes that kids can find the strength to overcome the problems in their lives.

He Said It

Finish strong. It is not where you start in life, but rather how you finish. It's that last play that can make all the difference in the outcome. Keep it simple: in everything you do, make your last rep your best rep.
—*Coming Back Stronger: Unleashing the hidden power of adversity,* 2010

Timeline

1979: Drew Brees is born in Dallas, Texas, on January 15

1986: Drew moves to Austin, Texas

1993: Drew attends Westlake High School

1994: Drew becomes a quarterback on the junior varsity team

1997: Drew enters Purdue University in Indiana

1998: Purdue Boilermakers win Alamo Bowl

1999: Drew meets his future wife Brittany on his birthday, January 15

2000: Boilermakers win Big Ten championship and play in the Rose Bowl

2001: San Diego Chargers choose Drew in NFL Draft

2003: Brees Dream Foundation is founded

2004: Drew is chosen for his first Pro-Bowl

2005: Drew seriously injures his shoulder; Hurricane Katrina strikes New Orleans and the Gulf Coast of the United States

2006: Drew signs six-year contract with New Orleans Saints

2008: Saints miss playoffs for second year running

2009: Drew and Brittany's son Baylen is born on January 15, Drew's birthday

2010: Saints win Super Bowl XLIV on February 7, and Drew is named Most Valuable Player of the Super Bowl Championship

2011: Drew sets a National Football League record with 5,476 passing yards

2012: Drew sets NFL record for most completions in a season with 468, breaking Peyton Manning's record of 450

2012: Drew signs a five-year contract with Saints for a record-breaking $100 million

2012: Drew made his 48th consecutive game with touchdown passes, breaking the record Johnny Unitas had held for 52 years

Glossary

adversity Misfortunes or challenges that stand in the way of happiness

bonus An extra payment

devastated Destroyed or ruined

dominant Most powerful or in charge

drafted Selected for service, for example on a sports team or into a military unit

football conference A league or division within a bigger group of teams. The New Orleans Saints are in the National Football Conference. Every season, the champion NFC team plays the champion team of the American Football Conference in the Super Bowl. The two conferences together form the National Football League.

foundation An organization that provides financial support

humanity The name for the race of human beings

ligament A tough tissue that holds joints together and connects bones

mentor A person who guides another person by teaching and supporting them

passing yard The number of yards gained by a team as they pass the ball

playoffs The tournament of games at the end of the season that decide which team goes to the Super Bowl

quarterback The team member in football who receives the ball to start the play and directs the offensive team (the players who are trying to score)

Roman numerals A numbering system from the times of ancient Rome, in which letters are used instead of figures. For example, X means 10, V means 5, and L stands for 50.

running back A player on the offensive team in a football game

scandal An event that shocks people

second-string Second choice, or backup to first choice

suspended Banned from working

touchdown A score achieved in football when the ball gets into the opponents' end zone

Find Out More

Books

Brees, Drew, with Chris Fabry. *Coming Back Stronger: Unleashing the hidden power of adversity*. Carol Stream, IL: Tyndale House, 2010.

DiPrimio, Pete. *Drew Brees* (Blue Banner Biography). Hockessin, DE: Mitchell Lane Publishers, 2010.

Websites

Drew Brees—the Brees Dream Foundation
www.drewbrees.com
Website of the Foundation with information about its many programs

New Orleans Saints
www.neworleanssaints.com
Official website of Drew Brees's team

National Football League
www.nfl.com/
Everything you want to know about the U.S. National Football League

Mardi Gras—National Geographic
http://video.nationalgeographic.com/video/ kids/history-kids/mardi-gras-kids
A look at New Orleans' most famous festival

Twitter

Follow Drew on Twitter
@drewbrees

Index

About the Authors

Sabrina Crewe has edited many series of educational books for young readers. She is the author or co-author of over 50 books, most recently *A History of the FBI* and a series about microscopic life. Adam Boehler grew up playing baseball in Livingston, Montana. He attended the University of Montana, where he studied journalism and creative writing.